WEATHER AND CLIMATE

SPRING

Priyanka Das

LIGHTBOX
openlightbox.com

LIGHTBOX

Go to
www.openlightbox.com
and enter this book's
unique code.

ACCESS CODE

LBXL9653

Lightbox is an all-inclusive digital solution for the teaching and learning of curriculum topics in an original, groundbreaking way. Lightbox is based on National Curriculum Standards.

STANDARD FEATURES OF LIGHTBOX

AUDIO High-quality narration using text-to-speech system

ACTIVITIES Printable PDFs that can be emailed and graded

SLIDESHOWS Pictorial overviews of key concepts

VIDEOS Embedded high-definition video clips

WEBLINKS Curated links to external, child-safe resources

TRANSPARENCIES Step-by-step layering of maps, diagrams, charts, and timelines

INTERACTIVE MAPS Interactive maps and aerial satellite imagery

QUIZZES Ten multiple choice questions that are automatically graded and emailed for teacher assessment

KEY WORDS Matching key concepts to their definitions

Contents

Spectacular Spring

Children can grow up to **three times faster** in spring than in winter.

More than **3,000** types of tulips **bloom** in spring.

The air grows warmer. Snow melts and the weather thaws. Winter gives way to spring.

Spring is a colorful season. The grass turns green and flowers bloom. Bright yellow and white daffodils are one of the first signs of spring. Tulips and hyacinths soon follow, bringing a rainbow of colors.

Many animals wake up in spring, after sleeping for months. The first warm days of spring bring out hedgehogs and ground squirrels.

What do you look forward to in spring? Does your family go for picnics? Perhaps you take your dog for long walks in the park. Some people go fishing or camping. Spring is a good time to enjoy the outdoors. Imagine how your perfect spring would look.

Spring in the United States

Spring lasts from about March to May. Southern states are usually warmer than northern states. More rain falls in eastern states than in most western states.

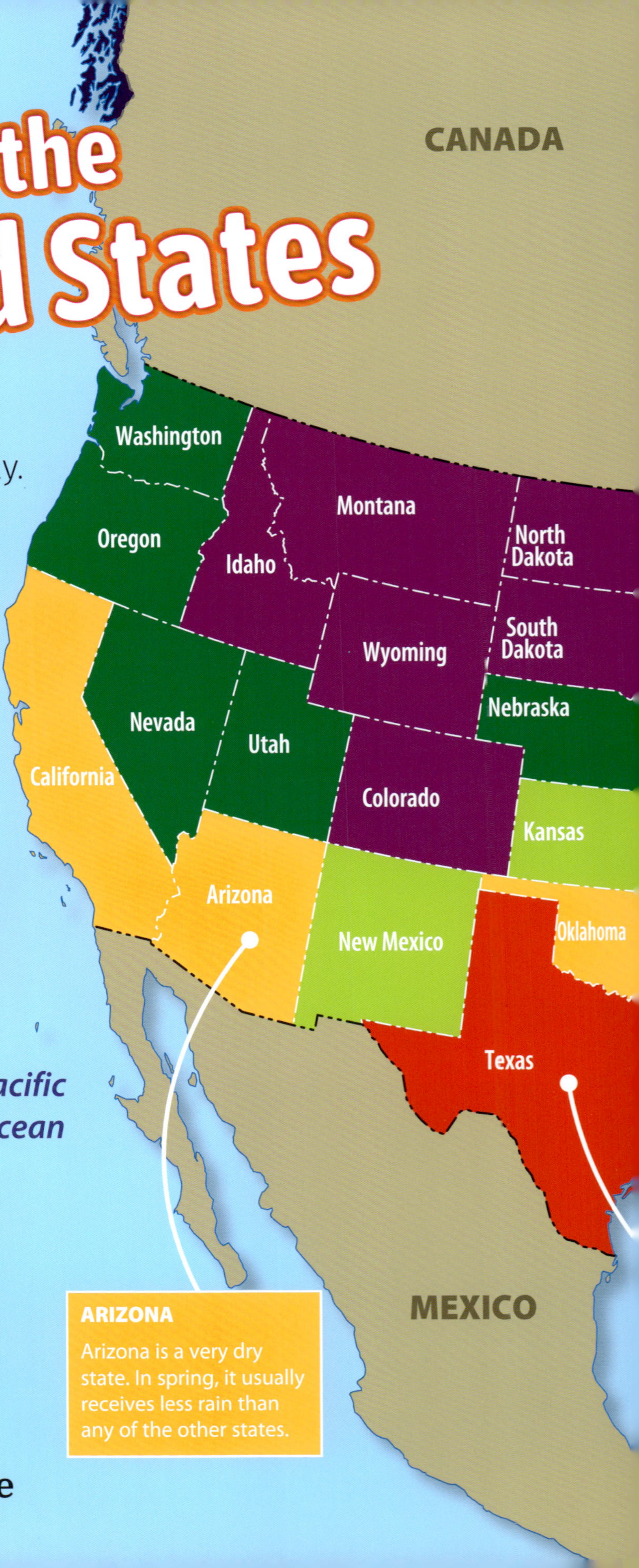

HAWAI'I

Hawai'i has the most spring rain of any state. It has the most yearly rainfall, too.

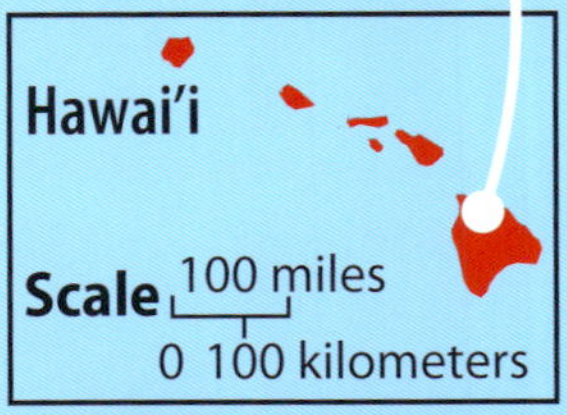

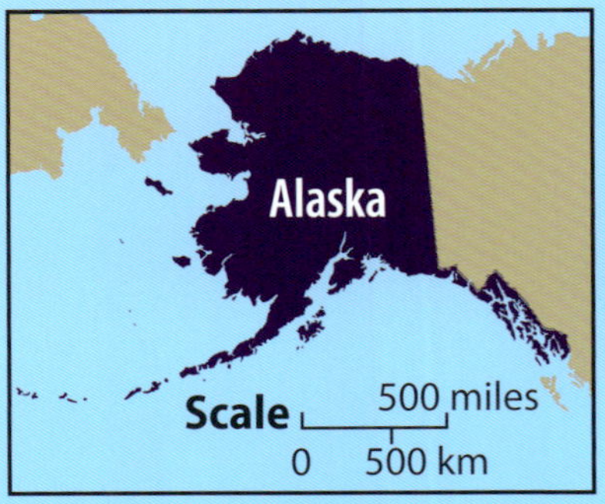

ARIZONA

Arizona is a very dry state. In spring, it usually receives less rain than any of the other states.

Can You Find Your State?

Find your state on the map. What color is it? Find the same color in the legend.

What is the average temperature of your state in spring?

Legend

Degrees Fahrenheit (°F)

- 20–30
- 30–40
- 40–45
- 45–50
- 50–55
- 55–60
- 60–65
- 65–70
- Other countries
- Water

Scale 0 250 miles / 250 km

FLORIDA

Spring in Florida is hotter than in any other state. Florida's average spring temperature is about 70° Fahrenheit (21°Celsius).

TEXAS

More tornadoes touch down in Texas than in any other state. More than half of these tornadoes are in spring.

The Weather in Spring

The year is divided into four seasons. As Earth moves around the Sun, the seasons change. Part of Earth leans toward the Sun. This part receives more of the Sun's energy. It heats up.

In summer and winter, half of Earth warms up. The other half cools down. In spring and fall, both halves are warmed a similar amount. Spring begins in the Northern **Hemisphere** in March. The spring **equinox** falls on March 21. On this day, the Sun shines directly on the **equator**. Day and night have nearly equal hours.

Earth's Seasons

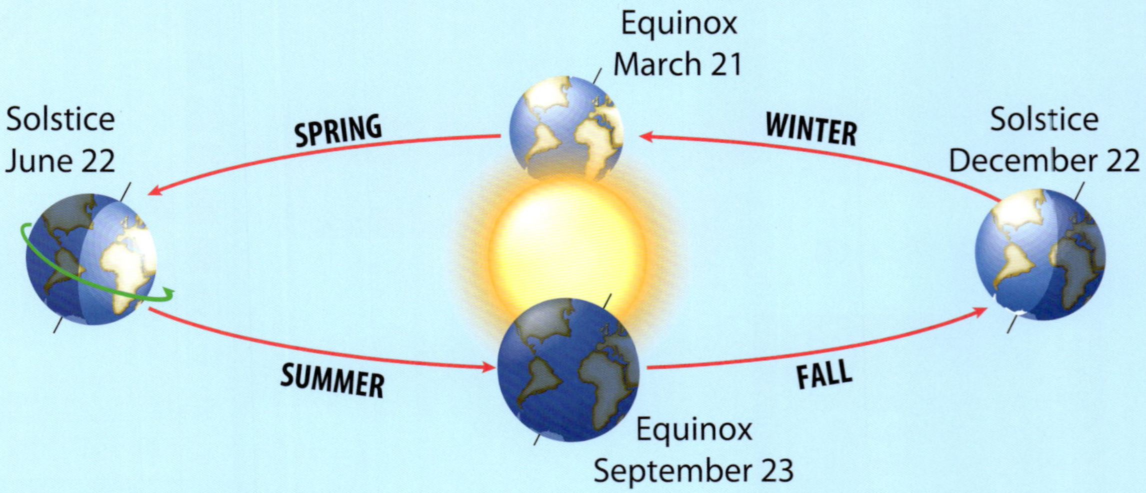

An Average Spring Season

From March to May, there are almost 800 hours of sunshine in San Diego, California.

Approximately how many hours of sunshine does Tampa get in a spring season? What about Syracuse and Dallas?

Which of these four states has the most rain and snow in spring? Which has the least?

= 100 hours

= 1 inch (2.5 centimeters)

The United States has about 1,200 tornadoes a year. This is more than the rest of the world put together.

Extreme Spring

Spring is usually a pleasant season. Temperatures are not too hot or cold. Many people think of spring as mild. However, spring can have extreme weather.

THUNDERSTORMS

Most thunderstorms occur in spring and summer. **Lightning** strikes rapidly. Power losses and forest fires are possible. Strong winds and heavy rains cause other weather **hazards**. Tornadoes and floods are often the result of thunderstorms.

TORNADOES

A tornado is a twisting column of air. It stretches from a thunderstorm to the ground. Tornadoes are the most extreme weather hazard in spring. The winds of a tornado can tear apart buildings.

FLOODS

Heavy rainfall and melting snow cause water to collect. Large amounts of water may result in floods. These great flows of water rise and spread over the land. Floods destroy property. People can drown. More people die from flooding than from tornadoes or lightning.

Extreme Spring Timeline

Every spring brings storms, tornadoes, and floods to the United States. The weather is very severe some years.

May 1889
The Johnstown flood occurs after days of rain. A **dam** near Johnstown, Pennsylvania, bursts. More than 2,000 people die.

March 1913
Heavy rains fall across Ohio. About 40,000 homes are flooded.

March 1925
The Tri-State Tornado hits Missouri, Illinois, and Indiana. It is the deadliest tornado in U.S. history. About 700 people die.

March 1942
Nearly 9 feet (2.7 meters) of rain falls on Hawai'i's Pu'u Kukui mountain. The event sets the U.S. record for rainfall in one month.

May 2013
A powerful tornado hits El Reno, Oklahoma. It is the widest tornado ever recorded.

April 2019
The Mississippi River overflows after heavy rains. Some areas of Davenport, Iowa, remain underwater for more than 50 days.

Weather Tools over Time

Scientists keep records of the weather. Studying weather patterns helps them **predict** what the weather will be like in the future. Many tools are used to measure the weather. Some are simple to make. Others are complicated and use advanced technology.

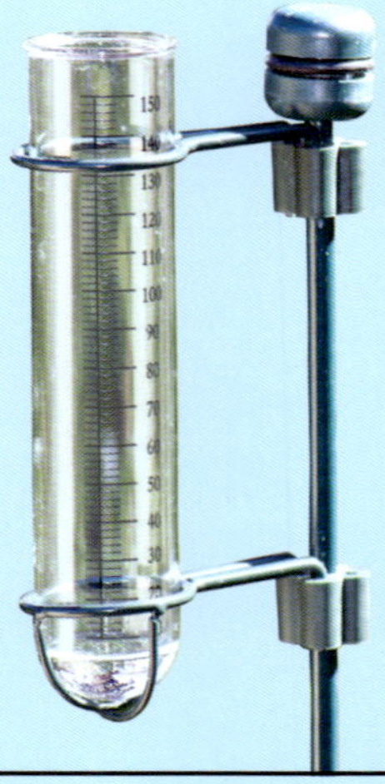

RAIN GAUGE

Rainfall is recorded in inches or millimeters. A rain gauge measures rainfall amounts. It collects water over a set period of time.

Christopher Wren helped build an early rain gauge in about 1662. He was an inventor.

DOPPLER RADAR

Doppler **radar** is used to find the structure of storms. It detects the movement of rain, hail, and snow. This helps track storms and tornadoes.

The Doppler radar is named after Christian Doppler. He was a physicist. In 1842, he showed how scientists could use light and sound waves to measure movement.

WEATHER MAP

A weather map shows weather conditions over a large area. It can display temperatures, wind speeds, storms, and more. Meteorologists use weather maps to help present information clearly.

In 1949, Clint Youle gave the first national U.S. weather forecast. He used a weather map to explain weather predictions.

Discover Scientists

Scientists want to understand the world around us. They try to find out why things happen. You can be a scientist, too. Learn about what different kinds of scientists do.

Inventors create new devices.

Physicists study **matter** and the forces that act on it.

Meteorologists study and predict the weather.

Spring Technology Today

Modern technology makes life more convenient. Spending time outdoors in spring is easier with the right tools. Technology helps people stay safe and connected.

WATERPROOF SMARTPHONES

Water damages electronics. Rain may ruin phones. Some coatings on phones resist water. Waterproof smartphones can be used when it is raining.

The coating on waterproof phones is a rubbery, glue-like substance that keeps water out.

PORTABLE SOLAR CHARGERS

Long camping trips are popular in spring. In many camping spots, electricity is not available. People charge their devices with power banks, or portable batteries, instead of electrical outlets. Portable solar chargers use the Sun's energy to charge devices.

Solar chargers do not usually run out of power because they can use the Sun's energy to recharge themselves.

WEATHER RADIOS

Storms and tornadoes often cause a loss of electricity. When cell phone towers are knocked down, phones do not work. Neither does the internet. Weather radios do not rely on cell phone towers. People can use them to communicate in emergencies.

One way that the government issues extreme weather alerts is through weather radios.

A Home to Withstand Tornadoes

Tornado-proof buildings are expensive and impractical. In areas with many tornadoes, most buildings are not tornado-proof. They have features to help resist medium tornadoes. Some homes have a storm shelter to protect families from severe tornadoes.

May has the **most tornadoes**. The United States averages **279 tornadoes** in May.

All **50 states** have had at least **one** tornado.

Shatter-resistant windows

Windows with shatter-resistant glass are stronger than regular windows. The glass does not easily break on impact. If it does break, pieces of glass will not fly around the house.

Reinforced concrete walls

Concrete is a strong, heavy building material. Steel rods **reinforce** thick concrete walls. Such walls can withstand powerful winds.

Solid steel doors

Wind cannot rip apart solid steel doors. Strong locks called deadbolts secure the door to the house. They prevent the door from being sucked into a tornado.

Storm shelter

A storm shelter is a safe room to stay in. Some storm shelters are part of the house. Others are underground. The walls and roof are made of reinforced concrete. There are no windows.

Tornado Safety

Learn what a tornado **siren** sounds like. If you hear it, take action right away. Get inside your house. Go with your family to a place that is safe from wind and flying objects. This could be any room without windows. If you have one, the basement is your best choice. Bathrooms or closets are other options. Plan in advance. Ask your parents what the safest spot would be.

Tornadoes may form unexpectedly. Know which places to avoid during a tornado.

If you are in a car, get out. A tornado can pick up a car. Run to a nearby building.

Do not stand near windows. Go to the basement or a room with no windows.

Do not stay outside. Go to a building. If there are no buildings near you, run to a ditch or a low spot. Lie flat, cover your head, and do not move.

Make a Rain Gauge

Meteorologists record how much rain falls in a place. You can build your own rain gauge to measure rainfall.

Items

2-liter plastic bottle
Scissors
Stones
Tape
Ruler
Marker or pen

Steps

1. Remove the bottle's cap.
2. Use the scissors to carefully cut off the top one-third of the bottle. Have an adult help you.
3. Place the stones at the bottom of the bottle. They will keep the bottle steady in a wind.
4. Turn the top of the bottle upside down like a funnel. Tape it inside the bottom part of the bottle.
5. Use the ruler and marker to make a vertical scale on the bottle. Mark the inches or millimeters. Your rain gauge is complete.

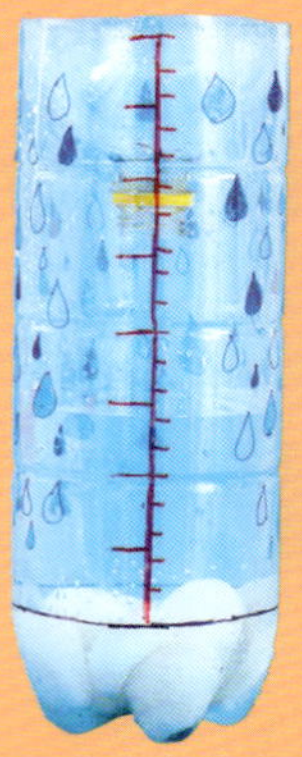

Leave the rain gauge outside on a rainy day. After 24 hours, go and check it. How high is the water level? The height tells you approximately how many inches of rain have fallen in the last day.

Spring around the World

POLAR CLIMATE ZONE

The polar zone is the coldest climate zone. Parts of this zone are covered in ice all year. The average temperature each month is below 50°F (10°C). Spring is very short in polar climates.

Wildlife: Arctic Fox, Arctic Wolf, Penguin, Polar Bear

TEMPERATE CLIMATE ZONE

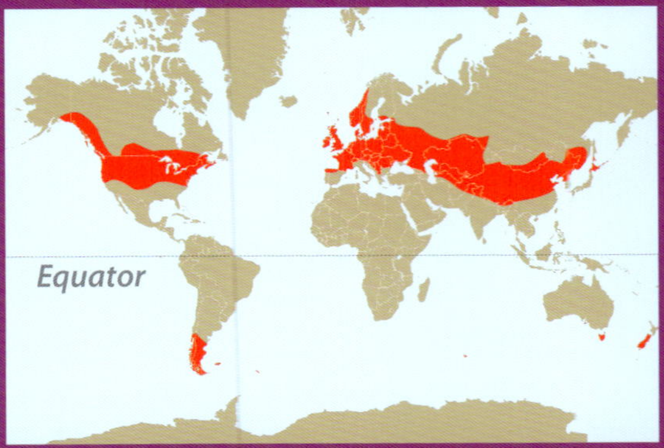

The temperate zone has four very different seasons. These are winter, spring, summer, and fall. Spring follows winter, the coldest season. Temperatures are mild in spring. The weather slowly becomes warmer. Eventually, spring ends and summer begins.

Wildlife: Giant Panda, Raccoon, Red Fox, Squirrel

Spring is different around the world. Places close to the equator are often hot all year. Areas far from the equator are cold. Earth has four major **climate** zones.

SUBTROPICAL CLIMATE ZONE

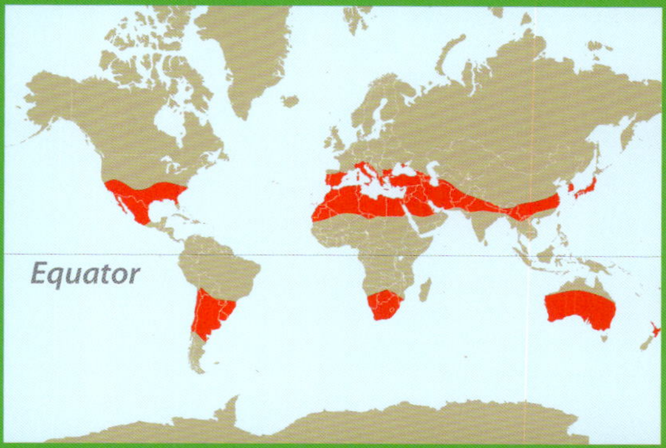

The subtropical zone has a warm or hot climate. Summer and winter are the two main seasons. Temperatures do not change very much from summer to winter. Spring is a short transition season between the two.

Wildlife: Alligator, Kangaroo, Leopard, Python

TROPICAL CLIMATE ZONE

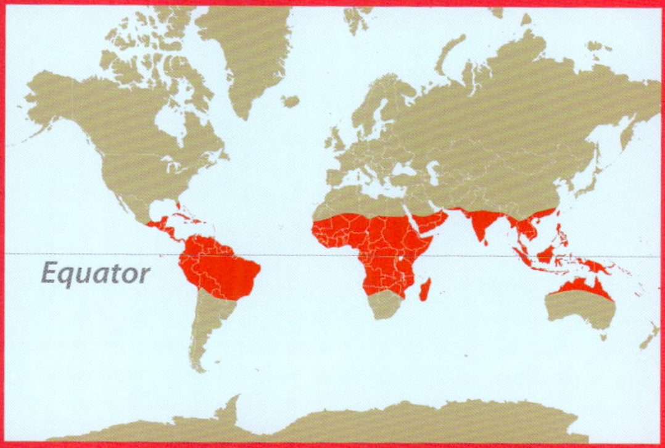

The tropical zone is the hottest climate zone. The weather is hot all year. Every month's average temperature is warmer than 64°F (18°C). Heavy rains fall. There is no spring season this close to the equator.

Wildlife: Gorilla, Komodo Dragon, Orangutan, Rhinoceros

Quiz

1 When is spring in the United States?

A: From about March to May

2 How many types of tulips bloom in spring?

A: More than 3,000

3 Which state has the most rain in spring?

A: Hawai'i

4 Which state experiences the most tornadoes?

A: Texas

5 Which weather hazard can cause both tornadoes and floods?

A: Thunderstorms

6 Where did the widest tornado ever recorded touch down?

A: El Reno, Oklahoma

7 When was the first national weather forecast in the United States?

A: 1949

8 What do physicists study?

A: Matter and the forces that act on it

9 How do solar chargers charge devices?

A: By using the Sun's energy

10 Which climate zone does not have spring at all?

A: Tropical climate zone

Key Words

climate: the average weather of an area over a period of time

dam: a barrier that collects or redirects flowing water

equator: an imaginary line that circles Earth, dividing it into northern and southern halves

equinox: when the Sun is directly over the equator and a day has equal hours of sunlight and darkness

hazards: possible sources of danger

hemisphere: one of two halves of Earth, especially above or below the equator

lightning: the passing of electricity from a cloud to the ground or to another cloud

matter: any object that has mass and takes up space

predict: to say that something will happen in the future

radar: a radio device that detects the position and movement of objects

reinforce: support something or make it stronger

siren: a loud, neighborhood-wide alarm that serves as a signal or warning

Index

LIGHTBOX

SUPPLEMENTARY RESOURCES

Click on the plus icon found in the bottom left corner of each spread to open additional teacher resources.

- Download and print the book's quizzes and activities
- Access curriculum correlations
- Explore additional web applications that enhance the Lightbox experience

LIGHTBOX DIGITAL TITLES

Packed full of integrated media

VIDEOS

INTERACTIVE MAPS

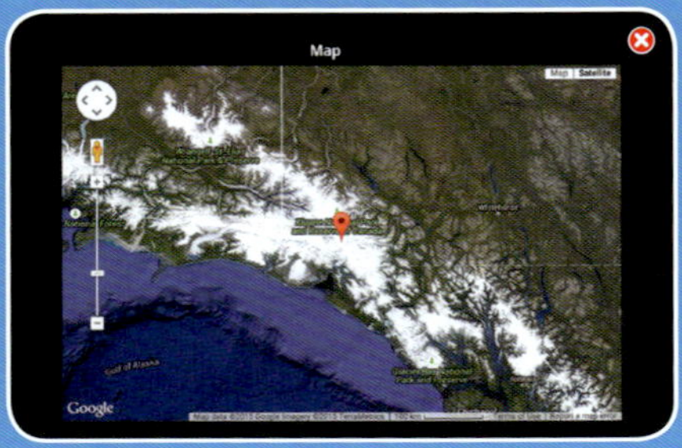

WEBLINKS

SLIDESHOWS

QUIZZES

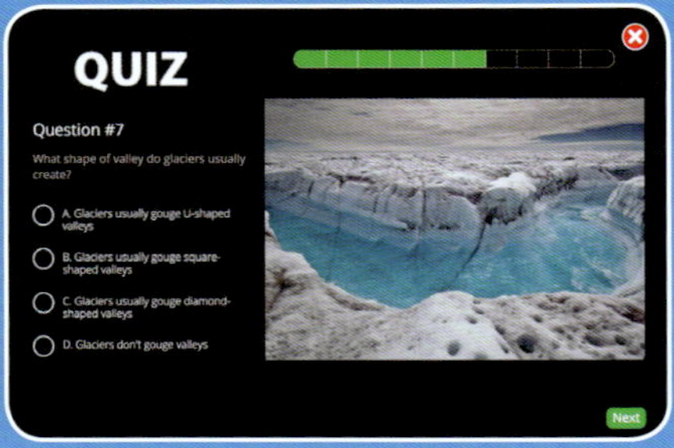

OPTIMIZED FOR

- ✓ TABLETS
- ✓ WHITEBOARDS
- ✓ COMPUTERS
- ✓ AND MUCH MORE!

Published by Smartbook Media Inc.
350 5th Avenue, 59th Floor New York, NY 10118
Website: www.openlightbox.com

Library of Congress Control Number: 2019942194

ISBN 978-1-5105-4515-1 (hardcover)
ISBN 978-1-5105-4516-8 (multi-user eBook)

Printed in Guangzhou, China
1 2 3 4 5 6 7 8 9 0 23 22 21 20 19

062019
122718

Project Coordinator: Priyanka Das
Designer: Ana María Vidal

Photo Credits
Every reasonable effort has been made to trace ownership and to obtain permission to reprint copyright material. The publisher would be pleased to have any errors or omissions brought to its attention so that they may be corrected in subsequent printings. The publisher acknowledges Getty Images, iStock, Shutterstock, Alamy, and Newscom as its primary image suppliers for this title.